FIRST FIELD GUIDE TO
SPIDERS & SCORPIONS
OF SOUTHERN AFRICA

TRACEY HAWTHORNE

Contents

Spiders and scorpions	4	How to use this book	11
Spider or insect?	6	Garden Orb-web Spiders	12
Collecting and keeping spiders and scorpions	6	Kite Spiders	13
		Garbage-line Spiders	14
A note on venoms	7	Tropical Tent Spider	15
Spider webs	8	Bark Spiders	16
How scorpions breed and grow	9	Golden Orb-web Spiders	17
How spiders breed and grow	10	Silver Marsh Spiders	18
Spider and scorpion taxonomy	10	Feather-legged Spiders	19
		Single-line-web Spiders	20
		Buckspoor Spiders	21
		Community Nest Spiders	22
		Velvet Spiders	23
		Grass Funnel-web Spiders	24
		Hackled-web Spiders	25
		Daddy-long-legs Spiders	26
		Brown Button Spider	27
		Black Button Spider	28
		Dew-drop Spiders	29
		False Button Spiders	30
		False House Button Spiders	31
		Net-casting Spider	32

Page 22

Page 54

Six-eyed Sand Spiders	46
Crab Spiders	47
Lynx Spiders	48
Cork-lid Trapdoor Spiders	49
Scorpion Spiders	50
Baboon Spiders	51
Thick-tailed Scorpions	52
Burrowing Scorpions	54
Rock Scorpions	55
Glossary	56
Index and checklist	57

Cannibal or Pirate Spiders	33
Long-legged Sac Spider	34
Mouse Spiders	35
Rain or Lizard-eating Spiders	36
White Ladies	37
Wheeling Spiders	38
Rock Huntsman Spiders	39
Violin Spiders	40
Burrowing Wolf Spiders	41
Fish-eating Spiders	42
Jumping Spiders	43
Spitting Spiders	44
Wall Spiders	45

Page 16

3

Spiders and scorpions

Why people assume that most spiders are fatally venomous is a mystery; although almost all spiders do produce venom and most can inflict bites, very few are dangerous to humans.

Spiders are highly adaptable, and are found in every habitat imaginable, from the seashore to the highest mountains. Many quietly share our environments and serve useful purposes, such as preying on the pests in the air, houses and gardens.

Most of the spiders and three of the scorpion genera in this book occur throughout southern Africa.

Different kinds of spider spin different kinds of web (see pages 8–9), and some don't spin any web at all. However, they all have silk glands and spinnerets[G]. Spiders spin several kinds of silk, each of which serves a different purpose. Some silks are amazingly strong – stronger than a steel fibre of the same thickness.

Spiders can be divided according to the methods they use to capture their prey. Some are web-builders and others are wanderers (which use their legs to catch prey). The web-builders ensnare their prey in their webs. Of the wanderers, there are some that 'fish' for their supper; others that pretend to be the ants on which they feed, holding up their front legs to look like antennae while they scurry about undetected among their prey; and yet others that sneak into other spiders' webs, where they feed on the spiders themselves or on the remains of their dinners.

Four scorpion families, Buthidae, Ischnuridae, Scorpionidae and Bothuridae, occur in southern Africa.

All scorpions possess venom. As a rule of thumb, scorpions with a thick tail and small pincers (e.g. *Parabuthus*) are more venomous than those with large, powerful pincers and thin tails (e.g. *Hadogenes*). *Parabuthus* are responsible for all the severe cases of envenomation in the region.

Aside from anything else, spiders have been on planet Earth for about 500 million years, and scorpions for about 400 million years, so for their advanced age alone they should be respected!

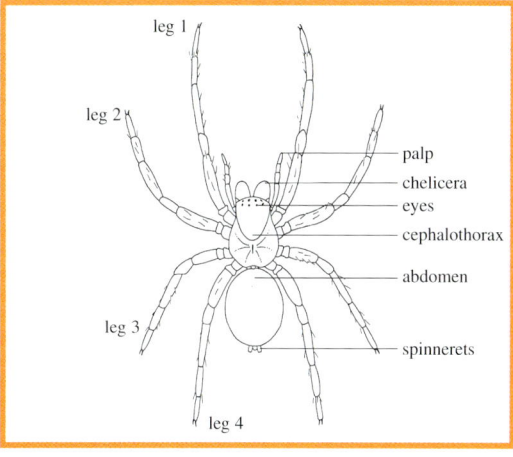

Spider

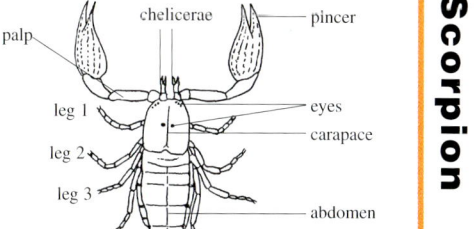

Scorpion

Spider or insect?

Although scorpions, with their pincers and long, segmented tails, are usually easy to recognise, some people find it hard to tell a spider from an insect. The following pointers should help:

- Spiders have two body parts (cephalothorax^G and abdomen^G; see page 5); insects have three (head, thorax and abdomen).
- Spiders have eight legs; insects have six.
- Spiders never have wings; insects usually have wings.
- Spiders never have antennae; insects always have antennae.
- Spiderlings usually resemble adults and grow by moulting; insect young usually do not resemble adults and grow by metamorphosis (changing form).

Collecting and keeping spiders and scorpions

You can find spiders in their natural habitats by sweeping grass and other vegetation with a butterfly net or by sifting leaf litter with a sieve. Also, look for them under stones and other objects, under bark and in rock crevices.

Spiders are very delicate creatures and are easily damaged. Never grip one by its leg, as the leg will almost certainly break off if you do. Rather, try to coax the spider gently into a jam jar with a small stick.

Live spiders can be kept in all sorts of containers, from a jam jar to a terrarium. Be sure to supply the spider with suitable food and water (and a good supply of air), and if you have caught a web-spinner, provide a wooden frame on which it can build its web.

Scorpions should be handled with care. The sting of southern African species rarely causes death in humans, but is extremely painful. Use long forceps to pick up a scorpion, grasping it firmly by the tail.

A note on venoms

Spiders

Very few of the 30 000 spider species known are harmful to humans. In southern Africa, the spiders to be wary of include Brown Button Spiders and Black Button Spiders, which have neurotoxic[G] venom; and Violin Spiders, Long-legged Sac Spiders and Six-eyed Sand Spiders, which have cytotoxic[G] venom. If you think you may have been bitten by a venomous spider, seek medical attention as soon as possible.

Page 55

Scorpions

All scorpions have neurotoxic[G] venom of varying degrees of toxicity. The dangerously venomous scorpions in southern Africa belong to the family Buthidae, recognisable by their thin pincers and broad tails. Three *Parabuthus* species are responsible for the small number of fatalities recorded annually. Some *Parabuthus* can spray venom; if this gets into your eyes it is best treated by rinsing with lots of clean water.

Page 51

Spider webs

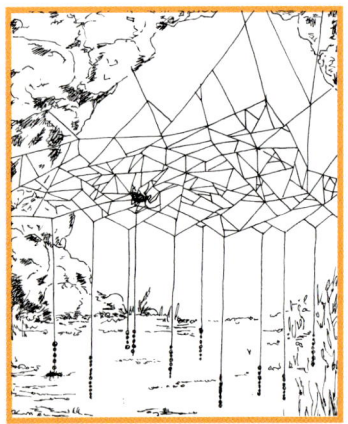

Space web (e.g. Button Spiders) Complex, three-dimensional structure, often called 'cobweb'.

Orb and orb-like webs (e.g. Garden Orb-web Spiders) What most people imagine when they think of a spider's web: a medium to large spiral web, spun across the flight path of insects.

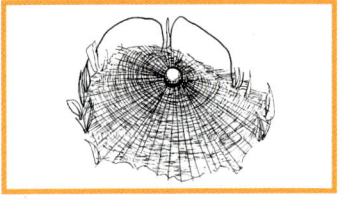

Funnel web (e.g. Grass Funnel-web Spiders). A funnel-shaped retreat region with a sheet extending outwards from the retreat; the spider hides in the retreat region and waits for prey to land on the sheet.

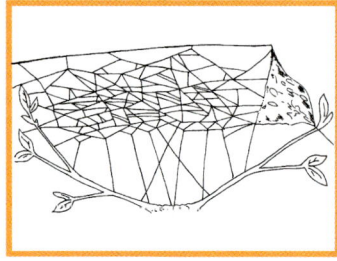

Community nest web (e.g. Community Nest Spiders). A large untidy 'nest' spun with cribellate[G] silk. It consists of a retreat of numerous tunnels and chambers, with catch webs set out at various angles.

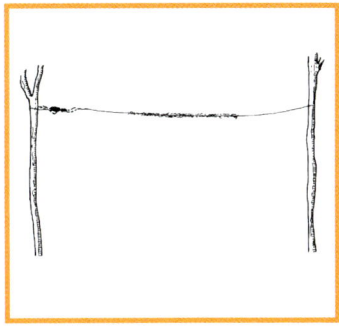

Ladder-like web (e.g. Hackled-web Spiders). When a moth or butterfly lands at the top of this web it will usually tumble down to the bottom – losing its scales along the way.

Single-line web (e.g. Single-line-web Spiders). A horizontal foundation line between the supports. The middle section of the line is covered with cribellate[G] silk and acts as a catch zone.

How scorpions breed and grow

During mating, the male scorpion grasps the female using his pincers and mouthparts. He manoeuvres the female to a place where he can deposit his sperm packet. This may take several minutes to several hours. He positions the female over his stick-like sperm packet, which then enters her genital opening.

Sperm is transferred to the female and fertilisation of the eggs takes place. The gestation[G] period takes from 3 to 18 months and, depending on the species, up to 90 young scorpions are born live. They stay in the care of the female for about two weeks. Some species take up to six years to reach sexual maturity.

How spiders breed and grow

Some female spiders have an unfortunate reputation for eating their mates after mating. To avoid ending up as dinner, male spiders of some species have evolved complex mating rituals. For example, the courtship of Jumping Spiders involves giving semaphore-like signals with the palps.

After mating, female spiders store sperm until it is needed to fertilize eggs. Spiderlings emerge from the eggs as miniature copies of their parents, and grow by moulting.

Most spiders do not care for their young, and some leave the eggs as soon as they're laid. But there are exceptions. The Wolf Spider carries the egg sac attached to her spinnerets[G] until the young hatch, then the spiderlings ride on her back. Fishing Spiders provide a nursery web in which the spiderlings can live in safety.

Many spiders disperse by 'ballooning' – they climb up a grass stem, wait for a gentle breeze, and then float away on a strand of silk.

Spider and scorpion taxonomy

In the classification of all living things, spiders and scorpions both fall into the class Arachnida. A class is divided into orders; an order can be divided into suborders and/or families; a family can be divided into subfamilies and/or genera; a genus is divided into species; and a species is a single type of creature. For example, the spider known as the Tropical Tent Spider is taxonomically classified as follows:

Class Arachnida
Order Araneae (spiders)
Suborder Araneomorpha
Family Araneidae (Orb-web Spiders)
Subfamily Cyrtophorinae (Tent-web Spiders)
Genus *Cyrtophora*
Species *citricola*

So the scientific name which identifies the Tropical Tent Spider is *Cyrtophora citricola*.

How to use this book

Each species account is split up into several headings, explained below.

Common name: The English name by which the spider or scorpion is known. In some cases an entire family or subfamily is known by a single common name, while in others individual species have been given their own common names.

Scientific name: This is its Latin name, always written in *italic* type.

Family/subfamily name: See page 10 for an explanation of taxonomy.

Afrikaans name: Where possible, the spider's or scorpion's Afrikaans name has been given.

Average size: This is the total length, measured from the front of the chelicerae[G] to the tip of the abdomen in spiders, or from the front of the head to the tip of the tail in scorpions. In the case of some spiders, the leg span is also given. In some cases, the lengths of the female (f) and the male (m) are given separately. Use the ruler on the outside back cover to give you an idea of how big the spider or scorpion is.

Identification: The general shape and colours of the creature.

Where found: The kinds of places where the spider or scorpion lives.

Habits: The spider's or scorpion's living habits (such as whether it is free-running or sedentary[G], diurnal[G] or nocturnal[G]), including whether it lives in a web and how it catches its prey.

Notes: Anything of special significance or interest.

Venom: The kind of venom produced by the spider or scorpion, and how it may affect humans, if it does.

Web: The kind of web the spider makes, if any.

Food: What the spider or scorpion eats.

Reproduction: How the spider or scorpion breeds.

Common species: Commonly seen members of the same genus.

Other genera: Because some spiders belong to large families, some have been grouped as such, and in these cases, the names of common members of the same family are provided.

Similar species: Other spiders or scorpions that may be mistaken for the species under discussion.

Garden Orb-web Spiders

Argiope

Family Araneidae; subfamily Argiopinae.

Afrikaans name: Tuinwawielwebspinnekoppe.

Average size: Length: f 7–24 mm; m 2–10 mm; leg span up to 80 mm.

Identification: Female usually silver and yellow with black markings, sometimes with ribbed abdomen[G]. Long, banded legs. Males usually small and plain.

Where found: Built-up areas; grass, low vegetation.

Habits: Diurnal[G]. Sedentary[G] and web-bound. Female hangs head-down in web, with two pairs of back and two pairs of front legs held together. Once prey is captured, spider wraps it in silk, then bites and kills victim. Sometimes prey is left hanging, wrapped in silk, until spider is hungry.

Notes: There are 12 African species in the genus. Larger specimens can inflict a painful bite.

Venom: Harmless to man.

Web: Huge, wheel-like orb web, up to 75 cm across, always with characteristic stabilimentum[G].

Food: Insects.

Reproduction: Male waits until female is feeding, then mates with her while she is distracted.

Common species: *Argiope australis*, *A. trifasciata*, *A. aurocincta*, *A. flavipalpis*.

Other genus: *Gea*.

Similar species: None.

Argiope australis

Kite Spiders

Gasteracantha

Family Araneidae; subfamily Gasteracanthinae.

Afrikaans name: Vliëerspinnekoppe.

Average size: Length: 5–15 mm.

Identification: Unmistakeable: brightly decorated with red, orange, yellow, white or black patterns; flattened, hard, shiny abdomen[G], usually wider than it is long, with a number of spiny horns on sides and back. Short legs. Male very plain and much smaller.

Where found: Forests; trees, bushes, plants.

Habits: Diurnal[G]. Sedentary[G] and web-bound. Female usually rests at hub of web. Once prey is captured, spider wraps it in silk before biting through to kill victim.

Notes: There are nine African species in the genus.

Venom: Harmless to man.

Web: Orb web.

Food: Insects.

Other genera: *Isoxya*, *Gastroxya*, *Hypsacantha*.

Similar species: Other spiders of subfamily Gasteracanthinae: Wedding Cake Spider (*Isoxya yatesi*) has raised ridges on abdomen[G]; Box Kite Spider (*Isoxya*) has squarish abdomen[G] and is duller in colour.

Gastercantha sanguinolenta

Garbage-line Spiders

Cyclosa

Family Araneidae; subfamily Araneinae.

Afrikaans name: Afval-lynspinnekoppe.

Average size: Length: 5–10 mm.

Identification: Mottled silver, black and grey. Long, lumpy abdomen[G], pointed towards rear. Short legs.

Where found: Forests; trees, bushes, low vegetation, grass. Common in open woodlands.

Habits: Diurnal[G]. Sedentary[G] and web-bound. Spider waits, hunched up and well camouflaged, for prey to alight on spirals of orb (stretched stabilimentum[G]). When disturbed, it seldom runs off but freezes instead, relying on camouflage to escape detection.

Notes: There are 14 African species in the genus. The common name derives from its unusual web.

Venom: Harmless to man.

Web: Orb web, with a 'garbage line' of debris (remains of prey, cast skins of spider and egg cases) down or across the centre.

Food: Insects.

Similar species: Web of Tropical Tent Spider (*Cyrtophora citricola*) similarly cluttered with 'debris' (actually disguised egg cases), but spider's abdomen[G] differs in shape; *Uloborus* spider webs also similar.

Cyclosa species

Tropical Tent Spider

Cyrtophora citricola

Family Araneidae; subfamily Cyrtophorinae.

Afrikaans name: Tropiese tentspinnekoppe.

Average size: Length: 8–15 mm.

Identification: Coloration varies, from cream to grey to black and white. Abdomen[G] longer than it is wide, with blunt, pimple-like protuberances arranged in pairs.

Where found: Built-up areas; trees, bushes, low vegetation near water. Common in gardens.

Cyrtophora citricola

Habits: Sedentary[G] and web-bound. Frequently forms large colonies. Usually hangs attached to debris and eggs in centre of web – a perfect camouflage.

Notes: There are seven African species in the genus. Sometimes known as 'Dome-web Spiders' on account of web shape, but unrelated to Hammock, Sheet or Dome-web Spiders (family Linyphiidae).

Venom: Harmless to man.

Web: Intricate, fine-meshed, horizontal orb web, surrounded by trip lines, often with egg cases and other debris woven in a line down the centre.

Food: Insects.

Reproduction: Elongate egg cases are attached to web, resembling debris seen in web of Garbage-line Spider.

Similar species: None.

Bark Spiders

Caerostris

Family Araneidae.

Afrikaans name: Basspinnekoppe.

Average size: Length: 8–22 mm; leg span: 25–35 mm.

Identification: Horny, wart-like projections on abdomen[G]; colouring imitates lichen and bark.

Where found: In and up trees, in webs between trees, on bark.

Habits: Sedentary[G]. Most species construct very large orb web, usually at night, then hang head-down in centre; they dismantle or abandon web during the day and rest up on small branch of thorn tree. (Diurnal[G] forest species does not dismantle web.) Rarely seen: superbly camouflaged, resembling nodule on branch.

Notes: There are nine African species in the genus.

Caerostris sexcuspidata

Venom: Harmless to man.

Web: Very large orb web (up to 1,5 m in diameter).

Food: Insects.

Similar species: Bird-dropping Spider (*Aethriscus*) is black and grey, resembling bird dropping; some Hairy Field Spiders (*Neoscona*) are very similar.

Golden Orb-web Spiders

Nephila

Family Tetragnathidae; subfamily Nephilinae.

Afrikaans name: Goue wawielwebspinnekoppe.

Average size: Length: f 13–40 mm; m ± 6 mm; leg span up to 80 mm.

Identification: Female larger than male. Elongated cylindrical abdomen[G] intricately patterned in black and yellow, blue or rufous. Extremely long legs, often with dense tufts of hair. Carapace[G] covered with silvery hairs.

Where found: Forests; trees, bushes, plants.

Habits: Diurnal[G]. Sedentary[G] and web-bound. Hangs head-down in hub of web, which is often strung with debris of old prey, resembling stabilimentum[G]. Smaller males often found in females' webs.

Notes: There are 11 African species in the genus. Webs can be so strong that small birds are caught in them.

Venom: Harmless to man.

Web: Huge, 'incomplete' yellow orb web (up to 1 m in diameter), characteristic of bushveld.

Food: Insects.

Reproduction: Female produces up to four egg sacs a season.

Common species: *Nephila senegalensis*, *N. pilipes*, *N. inaurata*.

Other genus: Hermit Spiders (*Nephilengys*).

Similar species: Silver Marsh Spiders (*Leucauge*) are smaller.

Nephila pilipes fenestrata

Silver Marsh Spiders

Leucauge

Family Tetragnathidae; subfamily Leucauginae.

Afrikaans name: Silwer vleispinnekoppe.

Average size: Length: f 6–15 mm; leg span up to 30 mm.

Identification: Long, cylindrical silvery or yellow abdomen[G] with bright red or green markings, pointed towards rear. Some species have very large jaws. Long, slender legs. Male slightly smaller than female.

Where found: In, on or under grass, usually near fresh water.

Habits: Often found away from web. Spins typical orb web in which it hangs upside-down. When not in web, hides by stretching out along grass stem.

Notes: There are 48 African species in the genus.

Venom: Harmless to man.

Web: Orb web.

Food: Insects.

Reproduction: Male's chelicerae[G] have strong spur used to hold female's jaws apart while mating takes place.

Similar species: Golden Orb-web Spiders *(Nephila)* are larger.

Leucauge species

Feather-legged Spiders

Uloborus

Family Uloboridae; subfamily Uloborinae.

Afrikaans name: Veerpootspinnekoppe.

Average size: Length: 5–8 mm.

Identification: Humped abdomen^G. Long front legs. Female *Uloborus plumipes* has brush of coarse, long hairs on first leg.

Where found: Built-up areas; trees, bushes, low vegetation. Often in and around houses.

Habits: Active day and night. Sedentary^G and web-bound. Sits in centre of web, hind legs drawn up and long, stout front legs held together and outstretched. Wraps captured prey in silk, then pours digestive enzymes on it to kill it.

Notes: There are 11 African species in the genus. Family Uloboridae is unique among spiders in not possessing venom glands.

Venom: None.

Web: Horizontal or obliquely-inclined cribellate^G orb web; hub often strengthened with stabilimentum^G.

Food: Insects.

Reproduction: Female lays eggs in neat cluster which she wraps in silk and guards until they hatch.

Other genera: *Philoponella*, *Zosis*.

Similar species: Spiders of family Araneidae, which spin similar orb webs.

Uloborus species

Single-line-web Spiders

Miagrammopes

Family Uloboridae; subfamily Miagrammopinae.

Afrikaans name: Enkellynwebspinnekoppe.

Average size: Length: 7–10 mm.

Identification: Long, narrow carapace^G; cylindrical abdomen^G which in some species extends beyond spinnerets^G in tail-like manner.

Where found: Bushes, plants, low vegetation.

Habits: Nocturnal^G. Sedentary^G. Spins single line of silk. Spider holds thread taut and jerks it suddenly when insect approaches, snagging prey. Rushes along line, wraps victim in silk, then pours digestive enzymes on it to kill it.

Notes: There are five African species in the genus. They are also known as 'Tropical Stick Spiders'. Spiders in family Uloboridae do not possess venom glands.

Venom: None.

Web: Single-line web, up to 3 m long, with cribellate^G section in middle.

Food: Insects.

Reproduction: Female carries cylindrical egg sac until spiderlings emerge.

Similar species: Other spiders of family Uloboridae.

Miagrammopes species

Buckspoor Spiders

Seothyra

Family Eresidae; subfamily Eresinae.

Afrikaans name: Bokspoorspinnekoppe.

Average size: Length: f 6–15 mm.

Identification: Robust, oval yellowish-brown abdomen[G], sometimes with faint cream or silvery markings. Covered in short, velvety hairs. 'Flat-faced' appearance. Legs short and robust. Male much smaller; markings may mimic certain ant or wasp species.

Where found: Dry, sandy areas in savannah and semi-desert.

Habits: Subterranean. Lives in silk-lined burrow in soft sand, the entrance of which is a flat web resembling a hoofprint, hence the common name.

Notes: There are 13 African species in the genus. The San are said to have used venom on arrowheads to kill prey.

Venom: Thought to be harmless to man.

Web: Mat of densely woven silk.

Food: Insects such as ants.

Other genera: Horned Velvet Spiders (*Dresserus*), Common Velvet Spiders (*Gandanameno*), Decorated Velvet Spiders (*Paradonea* and *Adonea*), Community Nest Spiders (*Stegodyphus*).

Similar species: Several others in the family Eresidae.

Seothyra species

Community Nest Spiders

Stegodyphus

Family Eresidae; subfamily Eresinae.

Afrikaans name: Versamelnesspinnekoppe.

Average size: Length: 4–23 mm.

Identification: Large pale grey to greyish-brown abdomen[G], covered with short, velvety hairs. Short, robust legs. Female usually larger than male, less brightly coloured.

Where found: Community nests attached to tree branches; solitary species found in or on grass.

Habits: A social species which attacks prey in groups and takes it back to colony for all to share.

Notes: There are 13 African species in the genus; two of these live communally; others may be solitary but live parasitically within community *Stegodyphus* webs. Possess cribellum[G] which produces frayed, woolly threads.

Venom: Harmless to man.

Web: Community nest surrounded by numerous catch webs.

Food: Insects.

Other genera: Buckspoor Spiders (*Seothyra*), Common Velvet Spiders (*Gandanameno*), Horned Velvet Spiders (*Dresserus*), Decorated Velvet Spiders (*Paradonea* and *Adonea*).

Similar species: Some others in the family Eresidae.

Stegodyphus dumicola

Velvet Spiders

Gandanameno and *Dresserus*

Family Eresidae; subfamily Eresinae.

Afrikaans name: Fluweelspinnekoppe.

Average size: Length: 12–18 mm.

Identification: Dark blackish-brown, covered with short, velvety hairs. Large, oval abdomen and short, robust legs. 'Flat-faced' appearance. Female usually larger than male.

Where found: Under stones; bark and trees.

Habits: *Dresserus*, often found under stones, is a sluggish species; *Gandanameno*, the tree-dwelling species, can be difficult to find in its maze-like web.

Notes: There are 25 African species of *Dresserus* and five of *Gandanameno*.

Venom: Harmless to man.

Web: *Dresserus* builds a messy, bluish-white, shroud-like retreat under stones; *Gandanameno* constructs a funnel-like retreat under loose bark, the entrance of which is often sheltered under a flat, solid, tarpaulin-like web.

Food: Insects.

Other genera: Decorated Velvet Spiders (*Paradonea* and *Adonea*), Community Nest Spiders (*Stegodyphus*), Buckspoor Spiders (*Seothyra*).

Similar species: Some others in the family Eresidae.

Gandanameno species

Grass Funnel-web Spiders

Olorunia

Family Agelenidae; subfamily Ageleninae.

Afrikaans name: Grastregterwebspinnekoppe.

Average size: Length: 7–13 mm.

Identification: Dark sooty-grey to mottled brown, with pale spots on long, hairy, tapering abdomen[G]. Long, slender, banded legs.

Where found: Built-up areas; in grass, under logs, in abandoned burrows of small animals.

Habits: Diurnal[G] and nocturnal[G]; shy and seldom seen. Sedentary[G]. Spins characteristic funnel web, which spider uses throughout its life, enlarging it as it grows. Prey landing on sheet part of web is quickly captured and dragged back into retreat.

Notes: There are two African species in the genus. They are abundant throughout southern Africa.

Venom: Harmless to man.

Web: Funnel web, made up of tubular retreat which opens out to form horizontal sheet.

Food: Insects.

Reproduction: Female lays disc-shaped egg cases in retreat parts of web or under rocks.

Other genera: House Funnel-web Spiders (*Tegenaria*), *Benoitia*, *Maimuna*, *Mistaria*.

Similar species: Wolf Spiders (family Lycosidae) have one pair of eyes very enlarged.

Olorunia species

Hackled-web Spiders

Family Dictynidae; subfamily Dictyninae.

Afrikaans name: Deurmekaarwebspinnekoppe.

Average size: Length: 3–5 mm.

Identification: High carapace[G], covered in white hairs; abdomen[G] usually decorated with light and dark patterns.

Where found: Forests; trees, bushes, plants. Common in gardens.

Habits: Sedentary[G] and web-bound. Diurnal[G]. Most species are solitary, but some construct communal web complexes. Some *Archaedictyna* live as kleptoparasites[G] in nests of Community Nest Spiders (*Stegodyphus*).

Notes: There are 10 African genera, containing 17 species, in the family.

Venom: Harmless to man.

Web: Ladder-like, made of network of irregular, cribellate[G] silk woven over the dry ends of twigs.

Food: Insects.

Other genera: *Anaxibia, Archaedictyna, Dictyna, Maimuna, Shango*.

Similar species: None.

Dictynidae

Daddy-long-legs Spiders

Pholcus and *Smeringopus*

Family Pholcidae.

Afrikaans name: Langbeenspinnekoppe.

Average size: Length: 2–10 mm; leg span up to 30 mm.

Identification: Grey-brown, elongated, cylindrical or globular abdomen^G, with darker chevron markings. Exceptionally long, slender legs.

Where found: Built-up areas; rocks, leaf litter, in holes and caves.

Habits: Sedentary^G and web-bound. Hangs upside-down under web. When threatened, spider vibrates vigorously, shaking web.

Notes: There are 88 African species in the family. Also known as 'mosquito eaters', they are useful in the home, preying on household pests.

Venom: Harmless to man.

Web: Loose, untidy space web in corners of houses and garages, and among rocks in veld and forest.

Food: Insects, such as ants and mosquitoes, and other spiders.

Reproduction: Female carries egg mass in mouth until eggs begin to hatch. In some species, female kills male after mating.

Other genus: Short-bellied Cellar Spiders (*Spermophora*).

Similar species: Spiders of the family Drymusidae.

Smeringopus species

Brown Button Spider

Latrodectus geometricus

Family Theridiidae.

Afrikaans name: Bruin knopiesspinnekop.

Average size: Length: f 8–14 mm, m 3 mm; leg span up to 40 mm.

Identification: Light cream to black. Globose abdomen[G] with characteristic orange-red hourglass pattern on underside; all specimens show a distinct pattern on upper surface of abdomen. Long, tapering legs.

Where found: Trees, stones, rocks, bushes, low vegetation, grass, leaf litter and rotting logs. Common around human habitation.

Habits: Sedentary[G]. Uses comb[G] to fling thread out to trap victim, then swathes prey in silk before delivering fatal bite.

Notes: There are nine African species in the genus.

Venom: Neurotoxic[G], causing intense localised pain. Not fatal.

Web: Space web, with retreat to one side and threads radiating from web to substrate[G].

Food: Insects.

Reproduction: Female lays spiky egg sacs, attached to web.

Other genera: Dew-drop Spiders (*Argyrodes*), False Button Spiders (*Steatoda*), House Spiders (*Theridion*).

Similar species: Black Button Spider (*Latrodectus indistinctus*) is black and lacks hourglass pattern below.

Latrodectus geometricus

Black Button Spider

Latrodectus indistinctus

Family Theridiidae.

Afrikaans name: Swart knopiesspinnekop.

Average size: Length: f 11–16 mm, m 3–4 mm; leg span up to 40 mm.

Identification: Black, globose abdomen[G] with dull red dot or stripe on upper surface. Long legs, with third pair shortest. Male brown, smaller than female.

Where found: Open veld; rocks, low vegetation, grass, leaf litter and rotting logs; wheatlands.

Habits: Nocturnal[G]. Sedentary[G] and web-bound. Shams death when threatened.

Notes: There are nine African species in the genus. Known as 'Black Widow Spider' for its habit of sometimes eating male after mating.

Venom: Strongly neurotoxic[G]; potentially fatal.

Web: Space web with retreat to one side and threads radiating from web to substrate[G].

Food: Insects such as beetles; geckos.

Reproduction: Makes smooth, round, pea-sized egg sacs.

Other genera: *Argyrodes*, *Steatoda*, *Theridion*.

Similar species: Black-phase Brown Button Spider (*Latrodectus geometricus*) has characteristic hourglass pattern on underside of abdomen[G]; False Button Spider (*Stateoda*) lacks ventral markings and has shorter legs.

Latrodectus indistinctus

Dew-drop Spiders

Argyrodes

Family Theridiidae; subfamily Argyrodinae.

Afrikaans name: Doudruppelspinnekoppe.

Average size: Length: 3–5 mm.

Identification: Conical, metallic-silver abdomen[G]; long, tapering legs with the third pair shortest and comb[G] on fourth leg.

Where found: Other spiders' webs.

Habits: Sedentary[G] and web-bound. Kleptoparasite[G], living in webs of other spiders, where it eats discarded prey remains; some species prey on the hosts themselves. Some species make a grating noise (stridulate) to attract mates.

Notes: There are 31 African species in the genus.

Venom: Harmless to man.

Web: None.

Food: Insects.

Other genera: Button Spiders (*Latrodectus*), False Button Spiders (*Steatoda*), House Spiders (*Theridion*).

Similar species: Some other spiders of family Theridiidae.

Argyrodes species

False Button Spiders

Steatoda

Family Theridiidae.

Afrikaans name: Valsknopiespinnekoppe.

Average size: Length: 5–15 mm.

Identification: Shiny black abdomen[G]; female sometimes has white band around front of abdomen; long, tapering legs with the third pair shortest and comb[G] on fourth leg.

Where found: Built-up areas and forests; trees, under stones, rocks, bushes, low vegetation, grass, leaf litter and rotting logs, disused holes.

Habits: Sedentary[G] and web-bound. Hangs upside-down in web spun close to ground. Makes a grating noise (stridulates) to attract mates.

Notes: There are 30 African species in the genus.

Venom: Harmless to man.

Web: Space web.

Food: Insects.

Other genera: Button Spiders (*Latrodectus*), Dew-drop Spiders (*Argyrodes*), False House Button Spiders (*Theridion*).

Similar species: Some other spiders of family Theridiidae.

Steatoda capensis

False House Button Spiders

Theridion

Family Theridiidae.

Afrikaans name: Valshuisknopiespinnekoppe.

Average size: Length: 6 mm.

Identification: Mottled brown or grey, globular abdomen^G; long, tapering legs with the third pair shortest and comb^G on fourth leg.

Theridion species

Where found: Built-up areas and forests; trees, under stones, rocks, bushes, low vegetation, grass, leaf litter and rotting logs, disused holes.

Habits: Sedentary^G and webbound. Hangs upside-down in web, into which remains of prey, stones and other debris are often woven.

Notes: *Theridion* is one of the largest spider genera, with 95 African species.

Venom: Harmless to man.

Web: Space web.

Food: Insects.

Reproduction: Female feeds spiderlings with regurgitated substance until after their first moult.

Other genera: Button Spiders (*Latrodectus*), False Button Spiders (*Steatoda*).

Similar species: Some other spiders of family Theridiidae.

Net-casting Spider

Menneus camelus

Family Deinopidae.

Afrikaans name: Netgooispinnekop.

Average size: Length: 12–30 mm.

Identification: Stick-like in appearance, with long body and very long legs. Female slightly larger than male, and has asymmetrical hump on abdomen[G]. Coloration resembles tree bark.

Where found: Built-up areas and forests; trees, bushes, low vegetation, grass. Frequently seen in houses.

Habits: Nocturnal[G]; rests on tree branch during day. Waits on grass stems or twigs near ground, holding web which it bodily throws over prey.

Notes: There are three African species in the genus *Menneus*.

Venom: Harmless to man.

Web: Scaffold web in which spider waits with rectangular, expandable cribellate[G] web (net) to capture prey passing below it.

Food: Insects – moths; spiders.

Other genera: Ogre-faced Spiders (*Deinopis*), Camel-back Spider (*Avellopsis capensis*).

Similar species: Other spiders in family Deinopidae.

Menneus camelus

Cannibal or Pirate Spiders

Ero and *Mimetus*

Family Mimetidae.

Afrikaans name: Roofspinnekoppe.

Average size: Length: 3–7 mm.

Identification: Shiny, yellowish body with dark markings; legs often banded. Egg-shaped carapace^G. Long, slender chelicerae^G. Spines on two long front legs.

Where found: Other spiders' webs.

Habits: Free-running; does not build web. Slow-moving, active at dawn and dusk. Preys on other spiders, such as Comb-footed Spiders (family Theriididae) and Hairy Field Spider (*Araneus*); some species also eat other spiders' eggs. Sometimes mimics web-plucking courtship behaviour of male host spiders to lure victim closer.

Notes: There are eight African species in the two genera. They are the terrorists of the spider world, sneaking into webs of other spiders, using the rake-like spines on their legs to immobilise their victims, injecting them with their quick-acting venom, and then dragging them off to be eaten.

Venom: Harmless to man.

Web: None.

Food: Spiders and their eggs; insects and larvae.

Similar species: Kleptoparasitic^G Dew-drop Spiders (*Argyrodes*) are also found in the webs of other spiders, mainly Golden Orb-web Spiders (*Nephila*), where they feed on discarded prey remains.

Mimetus species

Long-legged Sac Spider

Cheiracanthium furculatum

Family Miturgidae.

Cheiracanthium furculatum

Afrikaans name: Langbeensakspinnekop.

Average size: Length: 10–16 mm.

Identification: 'Black-faced' appearance characteristic. Long legs. Short, stout, black chelicerae[G].

Where found: Built-up areas and forests; bark, stones, bushes, low vegetation, flowers, leaves, leaf litter and rotting logs. Often found in citrus trees, strawberries and cotton; also in houses, where spins retreat sac in fabric folds.

Habits: Free-running. Agile, aggressive hunter, leaping on prey.

Notes: It is these spiders that are responsible for most cytotoxic[G] bites in southern Africa, as they crawl over sleeping humans. Bite is not initially painful.

Venom: Cytotoxic[G], causing inflammation and ulceration, fever and headache; wounds slow to heal, sometimes leading to secondary infections.

Web: None.

Food: Insects.

Reproduction: Egg sac similar to retreat, but smaller and denser.

Other genera: *Griswoldia, Parapostenus, Phanotea, Syrisca*.

Similar species: Some Sac Spiders (family Clubionidae) have maroonish chelicerae[G] and shorter first pair of legs; Mouse Spider (family Gnaphosidae).

Mouse Spiders

Family Gnaphosidae.

Afrikaans name: Muisspinnekoppe.

Average size: Length: 3–17 mm.

Identification: Elongated, oval abdomen[G], which may be uniform grey to dark brown in colour or decorated with bands and other markings. Short, stout legs.

Gnaphosidae

Where found: Grasslands, woodlands and built-up areas; under stones and other debris.

Habits: Nocturnal[G]. Free-running; may construct silk retreat under stone but does not spin web. Catches prey by speed and force.

Notes: There are 319 African species in the family. Sometimes known as 'Flat-bellied Ground Spiders'.

Venom: Harmless to man.

Web: None.

Food: Insects such as ants and termites; spiders.

Common genera: *Asemesthes*, *Drassodes*, *Setaphis*, *Zelotes*.

Similar species: Sac Spiders (*Cheiracanthium*) are lighter in colour; Ant-like Sac Spiders (family Corinnidae), sometimes called 'Dark Sac Spiders', imitate ants and wingless wasps.

Rain or Lizard-eating Spiders

Palystes and *Parapalystes*

Family Heteropodidae.

Afrikaans name: Reenspinnekoppe.

Average size: Length: up to 30 mm; leg span up to 110 mm.

Identification: Large. Dark brown to greyish, with slightly darker markings on abdomen[G]. Carapace[G] covered with fine hairs. Long, robust legs banded yellow and dark brown below.

Where found: Widely distributed. Mainly on plants; also rocks, leaf litter and rotting logs. Often seen around human habitation.

Habits: Nocturnal[G]. Free-running; does not construct web. In defence, front legs are raised high over head, showing dense brush of red hairs on chelicerae[G].

Notes: There are 14 African species in the genus.

Venom: Usually harmless to man but can cause toxic reactions in some people.

Web: None.

Food: Insects such as crickets; geckos.

Reproduction: Large balls of papery white silk and leaves built for egg sac; female remains nearby to protect eggs and spiderlings.

Other genera: *Panaretella*, *Pseudomicrommata*.

Similar species: Baboon Spiders (family Theraphosidae) lack yellow and black banding on legs and are never found on walls in houses.

Parapalystes species

White Ladies

Leucorchestris

Family Heteropodidae.

Afrikaans name: Wit dames.

Average size: Length: 15–28 mm; leg span up to 90 mm.

Identification: Large. Coloration varies, from whitish to cream, brown and clay-yellow. Carapace^G longer than it is wide, covered with fine straw-grey to light brown hairs. Long, robust legs armed with spines.

Where found: Dune areas of Namib desert and north-western Cape.

Habits: Nocturnal^G. Free-running. Lives in trapdoor tunnel in loose sand. Common name 'Dancing White Lady' due to frenzied, prancing hunting behaviour.

Notes: There are eight African species in the genus.

Venom: Harmless to man.

Web: None.

Food: Insects such as desert crickets; spiders; geckos.

Other genera: Forest Huntsman Spiders (*Panaretella*), Rain or Lizard-eating Spiders (*Palystes*), Rock Huntsman Spiders (*Olios*), Wheeling Spiders (*Carparachne*), Grass Spiders (*Pseudomicrommata*).

Similar species: Other spiders of family Heteropodidae, particularly Wheeling Spiders (*Carparachne*), but these are smaller.

Leucorchestris species

Wheeling Spiders

Carparachne

Family Heteropodidae.

Afrikaans name: Goue dame spinnekoppe.

Average size: Length: 18–24 mm; leg span up to 70 mm.

Identification: Pale off-white. Carapace[G] longer than it is wide, covered with fine straw-grey to light brown hairs. Long, robust legs, armed with spines.

Where found: Endemic[G] to dunes of Namib desert.

Habits: Free-running. Lives in deep trapdoor tunnel. Escapes danger by 'cartwheeling' down sand dunes, hence common name.

Notes: There are two African species in the genus.

Venom: Harmless to man.

Web: None.

Food: Insects such as crickets; geckos.

Other genera: Forest Huntsman Spiders (*Panaretella*), Rain or Lizard-eating Spiders (*Palystes*), Rock Huntsman Spiders (*Olios*), White Ladies (*Leucorchestris*), Grass Spiders (*Pseudo-micrommata*).

Similar species: Other spiders in family Heteropodidae, particularly White Ladies (*Leucorchestris*), which are larger.

Carparachne species

Rock Huntsman Spiders

Olios

Family Heteropodidae.

Afrikaans name: Jagterspinnekoppe.

Average size: Length: 8–15 mm.

Identification: Small. Yellowish to pale greenish, with slightly darker markings on abdomen[G].

Where found: Built-up areas; stones, rocks, bushes, low vegetation, grass; also other spiders' webs.

Habits: Nocturnal[G]. Free-running; does not construct web but weaves silk retreat between leaves.

Notes: There are 75 African species in the genus. Some *Olios* species cohabit with Community Nest Spiders (family Eresidae), feeding on insects trapped in hosts' web.

Venom: Harmless to man.

Web: None.

Food: Insects.

Other genera: White Ladies (*Leucorchestris*), Wheeling Spiders (*Carparachne*), Grass Spiders (*Pseudomicrommata*).

Similar species: Other spiders of family Heteropodidae, although most of these are much larger.

Olios species

Violin Spiders

Loxosceles

Family Sicariidae; subfamily Loxoscelinae.

Afrikaans name: Vioolspinnekoppe.

Average size: Length: 8–15 mm; leg span up to 100 mm.

Identification: Golden-yellow or reddish-brown with contrasting darker markings. Violin-shaped marking on carapace[G]. Six eyes.

Where found: Widely distributed. In built-up areas, in dark nooks and crannies and under floors; in forests, under bark, leaf litter, rotting logs. Often found beneath stones and in hollows such as old termite nests.

Habits: Nocturnal[G]. Free-running; does not make web.

Notes: There are 15 African species in the genus. One species is common in houses. Fangs very small; bite rarely, if ever, felt.

Venom: Cytotoxic[G]. Not lethal, but bite produces a mildly painful, ulcerated wound. Most victims are bitten at night while asleep.

Web: None.

Food: Insects such as fishmoths.

Common species: *Loxosceles spiniceps*, *L. pilosa*, *L. bergeri*, *L. parrami*.

Similar species: Daddy-long-legs Spiders (*Pholcus* and *Smeringopus*) are web-bound and vibrate web vigorously when disturbed; Spitting Spiders (*Scytodes*) have shorter legs and domed carapace[G].

Loxosceles species

Burrowing Wolf Spiders

Geolycosa and *Lycosa*

Family Lycosidae.

Afrikaans name: Grawende Wolfspinnekoppe.

Average size: Length: 6–30 mm.

Identification: Colours blend with environment: creamy brown or grey, with symmetrical markings on abdomen[G]. Radiating pattern on head. Characteristic eye pattern.

Where found: Common throughout region. Under stones and on or under sand, rocks, leaf litter and rotting logs; garden lawns.

Habits: Mostly nocturnal[G]. Free-ranging. Builds silk-lined burrow. Appears sluggish, but is capable of surprising speed; lies in wait and runs down or ambushes prey.

Notes: There are 22 African species in the genus. Easy to see at night, as eyes reflect bright green in torchlight.

Venom: Harmless to man.

Web: None.

Food: Insects.

Reproduction: Female carries egg sac attached to spinnerets[G] until spiderlings hatch, then they ride on mother's back.

Other genera: Funnel-web Wolf Spiders (*Hippasa*), Sand Wolf Spiders (*Pardosa*).

Similar species: Tropical Wolf Spiders (*Ctenus*) have different eye pattern.

Lycosa species

Fish-eating Spiders

Thalassius

Family Pisauridae; subfamily Thalassinae.

Afrikaans name: Visvangerspinnekoppe.

Average size: Length: 15–30 mm; leg span up to 70 mm.

Identification: Robust. Elongated, tapering abdomen^G, usually dark in colour, with various colours and patterns, often with white band around edge of carapace^G and on abdomen.

Where found: Near and on freshwater streams and ponds.

Habits: Diurnal^G. Free-running and fast-moving. Stands with long legs spread out, equally spaced and encircling whole body. Hunts along water's surface, diving to grab prey.

Notes: There are 15 African species in the genus.

Venom: Harmless to man.

Web: None.

Food: Insects, shrimps; tadpoles, small frogs and fish.

Reproduction: Female carries egg sac until spiderlings hatch, then guards young in 'nursery' among leaves.

Other genus: *Dolomedes*.

Similar species: Others in the family Pisauridae.

Thalassius species

Jumping Spiders

Family Salticidae.

Afrikaans name: Springspinnekoppe.

Average size: Length: 4–17 mm.

Identification: An attractive and interesting family. Usually black and white or grey and white; sometimes brown or brown and white. Often hairy. 'Flat-faced' appearance. Male usually more brightly coloured than female.

Where found: In almost every environment; often on dry leaves and wood, and on walls and ceilings of houses.

Habits: Diurnal[G]. Bold and curious. Hunts prey using excellent vision; stalks and pounces. Some species (*Myrmarachne*) imitate ants. Does not spin web; plays out strand of silk when leaping on prey, using this as 'drawback line'. Retreats at night into crack or crevice; seals itself into opaque, silk, sac-like nest.

Salticidae

Notes: This is the largest family in the order, containing 622 African species. Hydraulic pressure 'lifts' spiders (they do not possess extender muscles in legs which would enable them to jump).

Venom: Harmless to man.

Web: None.

Food: Insects.

Reproduction: Male signals to female with semaphore-like movements of front legs. Female lays eggs in silken cocoon which she guards until spiderlings have hatched.

Similar species: None.

Spitting Spiders

Scytodes

Family Scytodidae.

Afrikaans name: Spoegspinnekoppe.

Average size: Length: 4–10 mm; leg span up to 30 mm.

Identification: Small and delicate, with long, slender legs. Dark brown or yellowish with dark, symmetrical markings on domed carapace^G. Six eyes arranged in three well-separated pairs. Female larger than male.

Where found: Built-up areas; on rocks and in crevices, under leaf litter and rotten logs.

Habits: Nocturnal^G. Free-ranging; does not construct web. Ejects sticky mixture of silk and venom onto prey, zigzagging strings of it over victim until it is pinned to substrate^G.

Notes: *Scytodes* is the only genus in this family; there are 56 African species in the genus. Excellent household companion, preying chiefly on fishmoths.

Venom: Harmless to man.

Web: None.

Food: Insects, mainly fishmoths in houses.

Reproduction: Female carries egg mass until spiderlings hatch.

Similar species: Violin spiders (*Loxosceles*) have flat carapace^G.

Scytodes species

Wall Spiders

Anyphops and *Selenops*

Family Selenopidae.

Afrikaans name: Muurkrapspinnekoppe.

Average size: Length: 6–23 mm.

Identification: Mottled in greys, browns and black. Flat-bodied; round to oval abdomen^G. Legs held sideways, crab-like; sometimes banded. Eight eyes, six in front row, two larger eyes behind in second row.

Where found: Built-up areas; on or under bark and rocks, in crevices. Often seen in houses and conspicuous on plain walls, but well camouflaged elsewhere, such as on trees and rocks. Hides in cracks.

Habits: Free-ranging. Extremely agile, moving quickly to run down prey.

Notes: There are 59 African species in *Anyphops* and 18 in *Selenops*. Also known as 'Flatties' for their flat-bodied appearance.

Anyphops capensis

Venom: Harmless to man.

Web: None.

Food: Insects such as moths, cockroaches, fishmoths.

Reproduction: Builds flat, papery egg cases on walls, poles or under bark.

Similar species: Large Huntsman Spiders (family Heteropodidae) also have eyes in two rows, but with four eyes in each; easily confused with members of the family Philodromidae and some species in the Thomisidae.

Six-eyed Sand Spiders

Sicarius

Family Sicariidae.

Sicarius species

Afrikaans name: Sesoogkrapspinnekoppe.

Average size: Length: 10–15 mm; leg span up to 60 mm.

Identification: Reddish-brown to yellow, with contrasting darker markings. Flattened carapace[G]. Six very small eyes. Body and legs covered with sickle-shaped setae[G]; legs held sideways, close to substrate[G].

Where found: Arid and semi-arid desert areas; in the Lowveld; in some coastal areas. Beneath rocks, buried in sand, in caves.

Habits: Nocturnal[G]. Sedentary[G], but can move very fast. Buries itself in sand, and camouflages itself with sand particles wedged between body setae[G]; prey is caught when it crawls over buried spider, which leaps up and bites it.

Notes: There are six African species in the genus. Also known as 'Self-burying Spider'. Related to Violin Spiders (*Loxosceles*), which also camouflage themselves with sand.

Venom: Strongly cytotoxic[G]; can be fatal.

Web: None.

Food: Insects.

Common species: *Sicarius hahnii* (North West Province and Namibia), *S. testaceus* (Cape), *S. albospinosus* (Namibia), *S. oweni* (Northern Province).

Similar species: May be confused with *Hirriusa* (Philodromidae) and *Anyphops* (Selenopidae).

Crab Spiders

Family Thomisidae.

Afrikaans name: Krapspinnekoppe.

Average size: Length: 3–23 mm; leg span up to 15 mm.

Identification: Colours blend with environment, often bright to match flowers. Flower-dwelling species have round, high abdomen[G], wider towards rear; grass-dwelling species have longer, narrower body. Male much smaller than female.

Where found: Flowers, plants, grass, leaves, in and under bark, under stones and rocks, on bushes.

Habits: Diurnal[G]. Does not spin web. Artful ambusher, waiting on plants to surprise prey, which is often much larger than itself.

Notes: There are 356 African species in the family. Can walk sideways, backwards and forwards.

Venom: Harmless to man.

Web: None.

Food: Insects such as flies, bees; other spiders.

Reproduction: In some flower-dwelling species, male selects subadult female and rides piggy-back on her until she moults to maturity; then mates with her. In other, ground-dwelling, species, male 'ties' female to the substrate[G] with strands of silk before mating.

Similar species: *Thomisus* and *Diara* (family Thomisidae).

Thomisidae; *Synema* species

Lynx Spiders

Oxyopes and *Peucetia*

Family Oxyopidae.

Afrikaans name: Tierspinnekoppe.

Average size: Length: *Oxyopes* 5–12 mm; *Peucetia* 10–23 mm, leg span up to 50 mm.

Identification: *Peucetia* usually brightly coloured (most common species are green with pink markings); *Oxyopes* yellow, fawn or brown. Long black spines on legs. Abdomen[G] tapers to a point behind.

Where found: Bushes, low vegetation, grass, flowers, leaves.

Habits: Free-running; does not build web. Has good vision. *Oxyopes* runs and leaps agilely through shrubs and bush; can leap up to 2 cm into air to catch flying insects. *Peucetia* is more sedentary[G].

Notes: There are 86 African species of *Oxyopes* and 15 of *Peucetia*. Common name comes from cat-like stalking behaviour when hunting prey.

Venom: Harmless to man.

Web: None.

Food: Insects.

Reproduction: Female attaches egg sacs to leaves or twigs with silk and guards them.

Other genus: Dome-head Lynx Spiders (*Hamataliwa*).

Similar species: Resembles some spiders of family Philodromidae.

Oxyopes species

Cork-lid Trapdoor Spiders

Stasimopus

Family Ctenizidae.

Afrikaans name: Valdeur-mygalmorph-spinnekoppe

Average size: Length: 15–43 mm.

Identification: Dark brown to reddish-black. Shiny, hairless carapace[G]. Spiny 'rake' (rastellum) at tip of jaw for digging. Shortish, robust legs covered with spines.

Where found: Widely distributed in southern Africa. Burrows in soil.

Habits: Nocturnal[G]. Sedentary[G] and slow-moving. Digs a silk-lined burrow 10–20 cm deep, with extremely well-camouflaged, cork-like trapdoor lid. Waits for prey at mouth of burrow, legs just sticking out from under half-open trapdoor.

Stasimopus species

Notes: This is the only genus in the family; there are 42 African species.

Venom: Harmless to man.

Web: None.

Food: Insects.

Similar species: Baboon Spiders (family Theraphosidae) are usually hairy; may be confused with the Idiopidae and Cyrtaucheniidae, which are also trapdoor spiders.

Scorpion Spiders

Platyoides

Family Trochanteriidae.

Afrikaans name: Skerpioenspinnekoppe.

Average size: Length: 4–9 mm.

Identification: Shiny red-brown or black to grey, sometimes with pale markings on abdomen[G]. Body extremely flattened. Can fold fourth pair of legs over body like scorpion – the only spider able to do so – which gives rise to common name.

Where found: Under bark and stones. Frequently in and around houses, often under plant containers on verandahs. Hides in crevices.

Habits: Nocturnal[G]. Free-ranging; does not spin a web.

Notes: This is the only genus in the family; there are 13 African species.

Venom: Harmless to man.

Web: None.

Food: Insects.

Similar species: Long-fanged Six-eyed Spiders (family Dysderidae) are smaller, paler and do not have a flattened abdomen[G].

Platyoides species

Baboon Spiders

Family Theraphosidae.

Afrikaans name: Bobbejaanspinnekoppe.

Average size: Length: 30–90 mm; leg span up to 120 mm.

Identification: Large, hairy. Colour varies according to species, from light brown to almost black. Thick legs and long, leg-like pedipalps^G. Spinnerets^G stick out beyond abdomen^G. Front legs show red hairs on chelicerae^G when raised.

Where found: In warm, arid areas, under stones or in clumps of grass. Also around houses.

Habits: Nocturnal^G. Lives in silk-lined burrow up to 40 cm deep or silk-lined chamber.

Notes: There are 162 African species in the family.

Venom: Bite very painful but venom only mildly toxic to man.

Web: None.

Food: Invertebrates.

Common genera: *Harpactira*, *Ceratogyrus*, *Harpactirella*, *Pterinochilus*.

Similar species: Rain or Lizard-eating Spiders (*Palystes*) have yellow and black banding on legs, and are more slender and agile; Lesser Baboon Spiders (family Barychelidae) are much smaller; Trapdoor Spiders (*Stasimopus*) are hairless.

Theraphosidae; *Harpactira atra*

Thick-tailed Scorpions

Uroplectes

Family Buthidae.

Afrikaans name: Dikstertskerpioene.

Average size: Length: 25–70 mm.

Identification: Often brightly coloured with pigmented areas. Small pincers, thick tail. Bump often visible on inside curve of sting.

Where found: Throughout region, from KwaZulu-Natal dune forests to the Namib. Under rocks, sand and loose tree bark, and in vegetation.

Notes: Responsible for most scorpion stings in southern Africa; more venomous than *Opisthophthalmus*.

Venom: Sting very painful but seldom requires medical attention.

Food: Insects, spiders and other small invertebrates.

Common species: *Uroplectes triangulifer* and *U. vittatus* (North-West Province, Limpopo Province, Mpumalanga, Gauteng); *U. carinatus* (as above and Cape Provinces); *U. olivaceus* (North-West Province, Limpopo Province, Mpumalanga, KwaZulu-Natal); *U. lineatus* (Western Cape); *U. planimanus* (Limpopo Province, North-West Province).

Similar genera: *Hottentotta, Lychas, Pseudolychas, Parabuthus, Karasbergia. H. arenaceus, H. conspersus* and *Parabuthus brevimanus* are comparable in size to *Uroplectes* species.

Uroplectes lineatus

Parabuthus

Family Buthidae.

Afrikaans name: Dikstertskerpioene.

Average size: Length: 40–180 mm.

Identification: Varies greatly from yellow to black. Last two tail segments blackened or darker in some species.

Parabuthus capensis

Where found: Throughout the region in areas that receive less than 600 mm of rainfall annually. More diverse in arid areas. Construct burrows in various places such as under stones and vegetation or in open ground.

Habits: May produce a sound by scraping the tip of the sting over the first two tail segments. A few species spray venom when extremely provoked.

Notes: Most serious stings can be attributed to this genus. *P. villosus*, the largest member of this family in the world, is diurnal[G].

Venom: Very potent venom. Responsible for a handful of deaths annually.

Food: Small to medium-sized insects and fellow arachnids.

Common species: *Parabuthus capensis, P. granulatus, P. villosus, P. transvaalicus..*

Similar genera: *Uroplectes, Hottentotta, Lychas, Pseudolychas, Karasbergia. Uroplectes* are found in a variety of habitats, often in dry areas.

Burrowing Scorpions

Opistophthalmus

Family Scorpionidae.

Afrikaans name: Grawendeskerpioene.

Average size: Length: up to 180 mm.

Identification: Varies from bright red to yellow to brown. Powerful pincers and relatively weak tail.

Where found: Throughout the region. Burrows in soil and under stones and fallen tree trunks (not in forests).

Habits: Lie in wait at the entrance to their burrows to catch prey that wanders past. All species construct burrows. Many can produce a hissing sound by rubbing the hairs on their mouthparts against the underside of the carapace^G.

Notes: Endemic^G genus with over 59 species, some with very specialized distributions. More diverse in arid areas.

Opistophthalmus wahlbergii

Venom: Sting painful, but seldom requires medical attention.

Food: Insects, spiders, small scorpions and other invertebrates.

Reproduction: Gestation^G period of up to a year. Female gives birth to between 5 and 90 live young, which disperse into adjacent habitats after moulting.

Common species: Shiny Burrowing Scorpion (*Opistophthalmus glabrifrons*); Granulated Burrowing Scorpion (*O. latimus*).

Similar genera: *Opistacanthus* and *Cheloctonus*.

Rock Scorpions

Hadogenes

Family Ischnuridae.

Afrikaans name: Rotsskerpioene.

Average size: Length: 50–210 mm.

Identification: Very flat in profile. Powerful pincers and long thin tail.

Where found: Restricted to rocky outcrops and mountain ranges (except high mountain peaks).

Habits: Occur only on rocks, never on other substrate.

Notes: There are 8 southern African species in the genus. *H. troglodytes* is the longest scorpion in the world; males attain a length of 210 mm. Males have longer tails than females.

Venom: Venom is so weak it is hardly ever used in defence.

Food: Invertebrates, including spiders and smaller scorpions. Can prey on small vertebrates such as mice and lizards.

Reproduction: One of the longest gestation[G] periods (18 months) of any invertebrate.

Common species:
Hadogenes phyllodes,
H. taeniurus,
H. tityrus,
H. troglodytes,
H. lawrencei.

Similar genera: *Opistacanthus* and *Cheloctonus*.

Hadogenes gunningi

Glossary

Abdomen The back part of the body, behind the cephalothorax.
Carapace The hard shield covering the top of the cephalothorax.
Cephalothorax The fused head and thorax of a spider.
Chelicerae The first pair of 'claws' on the cephalothorax, used for biting, chewing and grasping (and including the fangs in spiders).
Comb Row of curved, serrated bristles on foot of fourth leg of spider.
Cribellum The plate-like structure with holes in it which lies in front of the spinnerets. It produces frayed, woolly cribellate silk.
Cribellate: Woolly silk that is produced from the cribellum. The silk acts like Velcro.
Cytotoxic Venom that attacks cells and tissues.
Diurnal Active by day.
Endemic A species whose range is confined to one region.
Gestation Development of the embryo inside the female's body.
Kleptoparasite (kleptoparasitic) A spider that lives on the food of another species of spider.
Neurotoxic Venom that interferes with the nervous system and causes it to malfunction.
Nocturnal Active by night.
Pedipalps The second pair of 'claws' on the cephalothorax.
Sedentary Moving about very little.
Setae Hair-like bristles covering spider.
Spinnerets The appendages on the abdomen through which the silk is produced.
Stabilimentum The special bands of silk across the centre of an orb web.
Substrate Basis or foundation (ground).

Photographic credits:

Norman Larsen with the exception of the following:
L Griffiths: pg 42.
J Leeming: pg 55.
John le Roy: pg 1 (right), 2, 17, 21, 22, 29, 38, 48.
A Pauw: front cover (top right), pg 3 (left), 26, 53, 54.

See: **www.scorpions.co.za**

The author acknowledges the kind assistance of Norman Larsen in the identification of photographs, and Dr Ansie Dippenaar for her contribution towards the scientific accuracy of the text.